SELF-DEFENSE OR
JIU-JITSU
ACHIEVABLE BY EVERYONE

MITSUYO MAEDA
or Conde Koma

前田光世

SELF-DEFENSE OR

JIU-JITSU

ACHIEVABLE BY EVERYONE

Ninety
Three

Original title: *Defensa personal o el Ju-Jiutsu al alcance de todos*
Edition copyright © 2022:
Ninety Three

Cover design and layout: Philipi Schneider

www.mitsuyo-maeda.com

Publisher's Cataloging-in-Publication Data

M184 Maeda, Mitsuyo. 1878-1941
      Self-defense or Jiu-Jitsu achievable by everyone/ Mitsuyo Maeda;
translated by Philipi Schneider; São José: Ninety Three, 2023. 174p.

     ISBN: 978-65-00-73123-1

     1. Jiu-Jitsu. 2. Self-defense I. Title.

CDD - 796
CDU - 796.853.25

Table of contents

Foreword to the English

edition

It is with great pleasure that we present to the English-speaking public, for the first time, an important historical record of martial arts, the book Self-defense or Jiu-Jitsu achievable by everyone, by Mitsuyo Maeda, which fills a major gap in the bibliography on the subject.

Maeda was an exceptional fighter. He spent much of his adult life spreading his martial art, by demonstrating, fighting, and teaching in several countries on two continents, eventually settling in Brazil and dedicating himself to the cause of Japanese immigration. Among his students in Brazil was Carlos Gracie, starting what would become Brazilian Jiu-Jitsu, which became a martial art in its own right and spread throughout the world.

This book was originally written in Spanish and published in El Salvador in 1913 by a publishing house called Tipografía Nacional under the title Defensa personal o el Ju-Jiutsu al alcance de todos. We have chosen to retain the already established spelling of Jiu-Jitsu in the title. In the original Spanish title, the spelling Ju-jiutsu appears, which is totally unusual and illustrates how difficult it is to transliterate the original Japanese word.

As Costa Rican historian Chester Urbina Gaitán writes in his article Orígenes del deporte moderno en El Salvador (1895 – 1921), Maeda traveled the country with a Japanese man known only as Nishimura. In a fight that took place on January 2, 1913, in the Salvadoran capital, San Salvador, Nishimura defeated a Cuban fighter named Pérez after five rounds. Meanwhile, Mitsuyo Maeda was teaching Jiu-Jitsu to the Presidential Staff at the Artillery Headquarters. The book, translated into Spanish by

Alberto García Dechent, was to be distributed in schools and used by the Salvadorean Army. Brazilian researcher and historian Fabio Quio Takao, in a review of the Spanish edition of the book, states that Nishimura is the man seen in the photographs in which Maeda demonstrates the techniques, playing the role of uke.

The work focuses on the self-defense aspects and makes no reference to martial arts as a competitive sport. It consists of a preface by Alberto García Dechent, the translator, followed by an introduction by Maeda himself, before proceeding to the presentation of the techniques, which is divided into six parts. In the first and second parts, some balance and calisthenics exercises are described, which are performed individually and with a partner, respectively. The third part is about self-defense techniques, in which various techniques are recognizable, such as the kotegaeshi widely used in Aikido, but also old forms of techniques that are still used today, such as the variant of seoi nage on page 74, which has been abolished in modern Judo as too harmful.

Next we have a short text by Maeda in which he talks about the importance of teaching pauses to the practitioner. In the text, it is noticeable that Maeda uses the term Judo to refer to his martial art, and then explains that this is the name used for modern Jiu-Jitsu. Although the term judo appears in publications dating back to the first decade of the 20th century, the identity of modern judo as a martial art distinct from ancient Jiu-Jitsu was not fully recognized until the 1950s. The poster advertising a Maeda fight on page 54 is a good example. In it, Maeda is introduced to the public as a representative of "Kano Jiu-Jitsu."

This brief section is followed by demonstrations of breakfalls, which the modern Judo practitioner will recognize as being some of the breakfalls or ukemis traditionally taught. The eighth section demonstrates some joint locks and chokeholds that will be familiar to judo and Jiu-Jitsu practitioners.

We did not intend to correct or add to Maeda's descriptions in the translation. The experienced Judo or Jiu-Jitsu practitioner will recognize the principles and techniques shown, and those that are not readily recognized deserve to be the subject of study and discussion in the dojo.

We have included a small biography of Mitsuyo Maeda with our edition. The accurate tracing of the history of a life is challenging. And in your case, even more so. Maeda has traveled much, fought much, and taught many. Historical records, with their fading tendency, hardly give an accurate picture of an eventful biography. Records are missing, information contradicts, and some accounts are distorted through the lens of myth. There is still much to be explored to get an accurate picture of the history of Mitsuyo Maeda himself and the development of modern martial arts. Outlining the exact individual contributions, separating factual history from mystification, rescuing the names of important forgotten characters — all this is still an incomplete task. And it is against this background that we have prepared this summary.

In conclusion, we reaffirm something that is already common sense — something that Maeda himself says in his introduction: you cannot master a martial art by studying only theoretical material. The proper method of learning involves constant practice under the supervision of a qualified instructor. The purpose for which we publish this book is not to provide a manual of self-defense, but to offer the public the rescue of an important historical work.

Philipi Schneider, publisher.

Mitsuyo Maeda, circa 1910.

Biography

Mitsuyo Maeda (前田 光世, Maeda Mitsuyo) was born on November 18, 1878 in the locality of Funazawa, in the city of Hirosaki, in the Aomori region, north of the island of Honshu, the largest island in the Japanese archipelago. He attended Kenritsu School Itiu (now Hirokou — a school in Hirosaki) and was known as Hideyo as a child. As a teenager, he trained sumo, but lacked the sturdy physique for this sport.

In 1894, at the age of seventeen, his parents sent him to Tokyo to apply to Waseda University. In the following year, he joined Kodokan, the institute founded by Jigoro Kano (1860 – 1938) in 1882. Jigoro Kano, who studied various styles of ancient Jiu-jitsu, compiled, and improved the old techniques, adding to the practice of the martial art a philosophical and pedagogical concern, founding Judo (柔道), whose name means "soft way".

He was only 5 feet and 4.57 inches tall and weighed about 142 pounds when he was assigned to Tsunejiro as a student. Tomita (1865 – 1937), one of the four Shitenno or four heavenly kings of the Kodokan, as four notable fighters of the early Kodokan were called. At that time, Tomita was the smallest Kodokan teacher. Nevertheless, in a fight that took place years earlier, in 1886, Tomita was able to defeat Hansuke Nakamura (1845 – 1897), a famous practitioner of ancient jiu-jitsu and representative of the old Ryōi school. Shintō-ryū, which was relatively large for the Japanese at that time.

Jigoro Kano in 1937.

Tsunejiro Tomita.

In 1899, Maeda was promoted to first dan black belt. On New Year's Day 1900, he was promoted to second dan. Promotion within a year was extremely rare. And from 1901, when he had already achieved the third dan, he took on the role of Judo teacher at Waseda University, the Army Children's School, the Gakushū-in, the Higher School of Teaching, and Ikkō College at the request of Jigoro Kano.

The spread of Jiu-jitsu in the Western world, which shaped Maeda's life, began much earlier. In 1879, to be precise, when the former American President Ulysses S. Grant (1822 – 1885) attended a Jiu-jitsu demonstration at the home of businessman Shibusawa Eiichi (1840-1931), at which Kano was also present.

In 1903, a senior Kodokan professor, Yoshiaki Yamashita (1865 – 1935) traveled to the United States, at the request of a Seattle businessman named Samuel Hill (1857 – 1931), better known as Sam Hill. Yamashita, who was the first judoka to reach tenth dan , began teaching Judo in the United States, teaching at the United States Naval Academy, even giving Judo lessons to then-President Theodore Roosevelt at the White House. Subsequently, Kodokan was asked to send more Judo teachers to continue Yamashita's project. In 1904, Tsunejiro Tomita , Mitsuyo Maeda and Soshihiro Satake (1880 – 1942) sailed from Yokohama to New York, arriving in the United States on December 8.

Early the following year, Tomita and Maeda gave a Judo demonstration at Princeton University and the Military Academy at West Point. In April of the same year, they founded a Judo academy in New York, at 1947 Broadway. Among them, there was a girl named Wilma Berger as students, who later, in 1909, in Chicago, gained space in the press when she used Jiu-

Jitsu to sell a robber who had attacked her by surprise.

On November 6, 1905, it is recorded that Mitsuyo Maeda visited Akitaro Ono in Asheville, North Carolina. Akitaro Ono (1876 – 1942) was a contemporary of Mitsuyo Maeda in the Kodokan and had arrived in the United States in May 1905, where he tried his luck in wrestling tournaments.

After this period in the United States, Maeda traveled to Europe. According to the Brazilian judoka Stanlei Virgílio in his biography of Mitsuyo Maeda (*Conde Koma – o Invencível Yondan da História*), he went first to Russia, later

Akitaro Ono on the cover of a French publication in 1908.

passing through Germany, France, Italy and England. In these various countries, Maeda, along with Satake and Ono, had several matches and demonstrations. Arriving in England, where he stayed for only two weeks, he already had fame and recognition as a fighter.

After his brief stay in England, he went to Belgium and then moved on to Spain, where he is said to have been nicknamed Count Koma. From there he went to Cuba and then embarked for Mexico, landing in the city of Veracruz on July 23, 1909. In January 1910, Maeda participated in a wrestling tournament in Mexico City, defeating Swedish wrestler and strongman Hjalmar Lundin (1870 – 1941) in the semifinals. In July 1910 he returned to Cuba, where he unsuccessfully tried to organize fights against two American fighters, wrestler Frank Gotch (1877 – 1917) and boxer Jack Johnson (1878

Hjalmar Lundin, circa 1913.

- 1946). On August 23, 1910, a fight took place in Havana between Maeda and a fighter named Jack Connell, which ended in a draw.

In 1911, Mitsuyo Maeda and Soshihiro Satake joined forces with Akitaro Ono and Ito Tokugoro. The four became known by the nickname "Four Kings of Cuba" because of the great success they achieved in their fights. In 1913, Maeda and Satake left Cuba and traveled through El Salvador, Costa Rica, Honduras, Panama, Colombia, Ecuador and Peru. While in El Salvador, this book was written. They then traveled through Panama, Peru, Chile, and Argentina until they arrived in Brazil in 1914. There are some contradictions in the records, as there are doubts whether he arrived first in Santos, on the coast of São Paulo, or in Porto-Alegre, the capital of the Brazilian state of Rio Grande do Sul. But it is known that Maeda and his company have traveled throughout Brazil. In an advertisement in the newspaper O Estado de São Paulo on July 19, 1914, a Japanese Jiu-jitsu instructor was looking for students in a room in the Liberdade district of São Paulo. The following year, the troupe came to Rio de Janeiro and performed at the Carlos Gomes Theater on May 1, 1915. A few days later, in an article in the newspaper *A Noite* in the May 15 edition, Maeda gave experimental Jiu-jitsu lessons to members of the Civil Guard in the Central Police building. They arrived in Manaus on December 18, 1915. Soon after, Maeda fought twice at the Polytheama Theater: on the 22

王　天　四　の　瑪　玖
（影撮春年五十四治明）

氏郎太長野大　氏郎四信竹佐　氏郎五德東伊　氏良光田前

Akitaro Ono, Soshihiro Satake, Tokugoro Ito and Mitsuyo Maeda
during their stay in Cuba, 1912.

against Satake and on the 24 against the boxer Adolpho Corbiniano from Barbados, which Maeda won in a few seconds.

A few days later, on January 8, 2016, Maeda travels to Liverpool with Okura and Shimitsu aboard the SS Antony. Maeda travels through Europe again, crossing England, Portugal, Spain and France, and returns to Brazil two years later, in 1917, where he settles in Belém do Pará.

After his return, Maeda fought only sporadically. The most famous of his fights was against a famous Brazilian capoeira fighter known as "Pé-de-Bola".

Jiu-Jitsu do Japão

Professor chegado ha pouco do Japão procura alumnos para ensinar, de accordo com os methodos japonezes, o meio de como devemos nos defender na rua dos ataques dos aggressores. Qualquer pessoa fraca, poderá se defender do outra mais forte, aprendendo os golpes de Jiu-Jitsu. Desenvolve também extraordinariamente o phisico; as pessoas fracas poderão, praticando o Jiu-Jitsu augmentar rapidamente a força e a resistencia. Trata-se á rua Conselheiro Furtado n. 57-A, das 18 horas ás 21 horas.

15

Advertisement published in the newspaper O Paiz, in Rio de Janeiro, on May 1, 1915.

Poster of Maeda's performance at the Politheama Theater in Belém, 1915.

Maeda, confident of his technique, would have even allowed the fighter, who surpassed Maeda in weight and height, to use a razor in the fight. Despite all the advantages, the capoeirista had to admit defeat.

It was during this period in Belém do Pará that Maeda's story met with the Gracies, giving birth to Brazilian Jiu-Jitsu. In 1917, Carlos Gracie (1902 – 1994), son of Gastão Gracie (1872 – 1912), a businessman of Scottish descent who worked in the rubber business. Carlos, then 15 years old, began taking lessons from Maeda and Jacyntho Sampaio Ferro, a local boxer and biker who became Maeda's assistant instructor. Carlos moved to Rio de Janeiro in 1921, starting to teach Jiu-Jitsu, including to his brothers, George Gracie (1911 – 1985), and Hélio Gracie (1913 – 2004), who was the youngest. George was the first Gracie family fighter to stand out in the fighting world, but it was Hélio who became his great ambassador. He honed the learned techniques for his slight

Os guardas cívis vão aprender o jiu-jitsu

Uma aula de experiencia na Policia Central

Excerpt from an article in the newspaper A Noite, from Rio de Janeiro, on May 19, 1915. The headline reads: "Civil guards will learn jiu-jitsu".

build, making them more efficient. This experience was the origin of Brazilian Jiu-Jitsu, which spread throughout the world.

In 1921, Meada founded his first Judo academy — possibly the first Judo academy in Brazil — at Clube do Remo, in the Cidade Velha district of Belém do Pará. Subsequently, the academy changed its location several times.

In 1924, while hospitalized for a kidney problem, Maeda met the English nurse Daysy May Iris, whom he eventually married and later adopted the girls Celeste and Clívia.

Maeda was naturalized as a Brazilian in 1927 and took the name Otávio Maeda.

During the 1920s, Maeda dedicated himself to Japanese immigration, serving as an interpreter and representative of the Japanese interest with the government of Pará. With the founding of the *Companhia Nipônica de Plantações do Brasil* (Nambei Takoshuku kabushiki Kaisha) in 1928, which had Maeda on its board, with the position of fiscal advisor, is that Japanese immigration to the Amazon began to gain strength.

Maeda continued to teach judo and was promoted to sixth dan in 1929 and seventh dan in 1941, posthumously, as he died of kidney disease in Belém on November 28, 1941.

In May 1956, a monument to Maeda was erected in his hometown of Hirosaki, Japan.

Mitsuyo Maeda's tomb, at the Santa Isabel cemetery, in Belém do Pará.

REFERENCES

(July 17, 1914). O Estado de S. Paulo. Accessed on September 4, 2022, available at https://acervo.estadao.com.br/pagina/#!/19140717-12992-nac-0001-999-1-not

(May 1, 1915). O Paiz (11163), 12. Accessed on September 4, 2022, available at http://memoria.bn.br/pdf/178691/per178691_1915_11163.pdf

Bunasawa, N., & Murray, J. (2018). The toughest man who ever lived: the story of Mitsuyo Maeda (4th ed.). Nevada: Judo Journal and Innovations, Inc.

Eastern Europe BJJ. (2020). Accessed on September 4, 2022, available at The Lost Legend of Jacyntho Ferro, One of Carlos Gracie Sr.'s Jiu-Jitsu Instructors: https://www.bjjee.com/articles/the-lost-legend-of-jacyntho--ferro-one-of-carlos-gracie-sr-s-jiu-jitsu-instructors/

Gaitán, C. U. (2006). Orígenes del deporte moderno. Source: efdeportes.com: http://www.efdeportes.com/efd97/salvador.htm

Laydner, L. O., & Takao, F. Q. (September 2, 2013). Maeda ensinava Jiu--jitsu no Rio 10 anos antes dos Gracies. Accessed on September 4, 2022, available at Pancadante: http://pancadante.weebly.com/maeda-ensinava--jiu-jitsu-no-rio-10-anos-antes-dos-gracies.html

O invencível Conde Koma que desafiou a luta contra a Amazônia. (2014). Source: 100 anos de Imigração Japonesa no Brasil: https://www.ndl.go.jp/brasil/pt/column/kodekoma.html

Os guardas civis vão aprender o jiu-jitsu. (May 1915). A noite (1221). Accessed on September 4, 2022, available at http://memoria.bn.br/pdf/348970/per348970_1915_01221.pdf

Takao, F. Q. (July 25, 2016). Novas imagens do Conde Koma - Resenha do livro "Defensa Personal O El Ju Jiutsu al alcance de todos". Source: https://blogs.oglobo.globo.com/mma/post/novas-imagens-do-conde-koma-resenha-do-livro-defensa-personal-o-el-ju-jiutsu-al-alcance-de-todos.html

Tsutsumi, G. (2020). Cultura Japonesa Vol. 8 – Conde Koma – disseminando a arte marcial japonesa no Brasil. Source: Jornal Nippak: https://www.jnippak.com.br/2020/cultura-japonesa-vol-8-conde-koma/

Virgílio, S. (2017). Conde Koma: o invencível Yondan da história (2nd ed.). Campinas, São Paulo: Átomo.

PREFACE

As a lover of all that has to do with the development of our physical, moral and intellectual culture, I have encouraged the popular Yamato Maida (Conde Koma), undefeated world champion in the difficult art of Jiu-jitsu, to publish this work in which he points out some of the many advantages of this art over other sports, especially in terms of self-defense.

The main objective of this book, then, is to offer our young enthusiasts a simple path to perfect physical development, which at the same time keeps them in excellent health and gives them invaluable means of defense in moments of real danger, from which no one is exempt.

If you follow the exercises we will show you later, you will be able to acquire the necessary knowledge to ward off any attack you fall victim to, you will achieve good muscle development and, in short, you will learn something that can be of real practical use.

It was in vain to get Conde Koma to write a complete treatise that can turn anyone who follows it into a jiu-jitsu expert. Professional Jiu-Jitsu, Conde said, is a hard and difficult art that cannot be learned so easily, and even if he tried to simplify it as much as possible to make it understandable for children, not everyone who reads this treatise would be able to perform these feats as they are described, because it would require many prerequisites. But you will have more success with what we propose, because it is certainly the most practical. The ability to defend yourself at any time certainly deserves to be studied carefully.

Before introducing you to certain techniques and dodges, we will show you some calisthenic exercises that you must follow strictly, without practicing one before the other, otherwise you will not get the desired benefit. They will tire you and bore you, but you must be persistent.

In general, most people do not lack the desire to achieve the results of physical culture, but they have a great aversion to the inevitable effort that requires intense and constant exercise. No one knows what he can do until he has tried it, and few try to do all they can until they are forced to do it.

So, in order to gain agility, dexterity, complete development, etc. , I advise you, as I said, to start with the first exercises, which are made known and correspond to what is written in the instructions; then he will then proceed with the defense practices, which he will try in the company of another enthusiast; if there are three, so much the better, because then there will be one who can criticize what the other two are doing, and excellent results will be obtained.

An extensive volume could be written about this art-science. However, we only have space for a few examples, the most practical and important ones.

Alberto García Dechent

Useful knowledge

If you try to practice with a friend some of the techniques we are going to present, you will find that in some of them you can easily free yourself from the grip of the other by using more force; but the use of too much force should be avoided as much as possible, and you should learn more scientific methods. Jiu-Jitsu, or what we propose to demonstrate, is, as we have already said, a science and does not require much physical strength, since it focuses more on maximum skill and agility than on brute force. This agility and the precise knowledge of numerous sensitive points in our human machine make this science the best known means of defense.

The effect produced in these sensitive points exposed to hits will certainly produce better results on many occasions than the use of violent methods.

Pressure with the fingers, blows with the tip of the duly hardened hand and with the fists, on the Adam's apple, on the junction of the nose and forehead, on the nose below the entrances, on the base of the skull or on the nape of the neck, on the mouth of the stomach or the solar plexus, in certain regions of the shoulder, above the elbow, in the tendons of the wrists, on the sides, with the knee in the groin and the genitals, and the twisting of the wrists, arms and legs represent, in part, the means of defense that jiu-jitsu offers and that can be used against bandits and people who stop at nothing.

But that's only part of what defense is about, and it's not just what Jiu-Jitsu encompasses.

If it is favorable for a person to know the protective procedures of this art, it is even more favorable for him to know properly the procedures that serve to preserve health, some of which are:

+ Light and nutritious food.
+ Fresh air.
+ Drink plenty of pure, cold or natural water, but not with ice.
+ Don't eat too much.
+ Don't eat too much meat.
+ Don't drink alcohol.
+ Don't smoke too much.
+ Avoid recklessness and excessive sexual activity.

A strong and healthy stomach is the foundation of health, and this is achieved simply by not abusing it, eating out of turn and giving it more work than it can naturally handle. Constipation and indigestion cause more disturbances in our bodies than almost all other causes combined, with the exception of the excessive use of sexual pleasures. Let us insert here some observations of Professor WJ Clark which largely agree with what we have been saying:

"The intestines, the colon and the rectum, are organs whose functions are to complete digestion, to absorb the assimilable part of food, and expelling waste. Its absorptive capacity is very large. Its tissues contain numerous blood vessels and nerves. Intestinal nerves play a highly complex role, acting on glands and blood vessels and producing absorption, secretion and peristalsis. They not only control the functions of the intestines, but

with the help of their brain centers, they exert an influence on all other brain centers, thus affecting the organism in general. It is evident that the retention of unassimilable residues to be excreted must have a harmful effect on the intestinal veins and nerves. Accumulations and blockages occur in the intestinal canal, the materials decompose and form toxins that poison the entire system, while the constant pressure exerted on the intestinal walls, where the blood vessels and nerves are located, in turn causes other disorders."

Constipation exerts a great influence on sexual functions, but while it is true that any influence which causes nervous disturbance will interfere with these functions, constipation does not interfere with them merely because of nerve transmissions. The seminal gland in man is located between the bladder and the rectum, and becomes irritated when subjected to constant pressure resulting from the occupancy of the rectum by food residue. It is the most common cause of juvenile excess and involuntary loss of vitality. As long as constipation persists, sexual functions cannot be normal.

Most pharmaceutical preparations are intestinal stimulants, and it must not be forgotten that every stimulation is accompanied by a reaction and that the excretory functions are weakened by the use of the said stimulants. Therefore, it is preferable to cure with reasonable means that not only improve health, will considerably increase vitality.

This means consists primarily in a proper diet, to which must be added proper gymnastics with leg movements and others, as we shall show below, whose movements bring the abdominal muscles into action, as well as massage of the region.

Poor digestion is often due to a lack of outdoor exercise. I'll conclude because I don't wish to tire the reader with further observations, as a simple exposition of the myriad of knowledge that Jiu-Jitsu encompasses would take up much space.

Note: I greatly appreciate comments from readers of this book on any question or exercises that are not adequately described. I understand that it was quite a difficult task for the translator to make these exercises and techniques as simple and understandable as possible, so I take the liberty of making this disclaimer.

Conde Koma

Simple exercises

These first five exercises we will show you are performed without any muscle contraction and in a normal resting state.

Figure 1

Put yourself in the position indicated by the picture, which we will call *"first position"*.

Then breathe in and out very slowly and deeply, as much air as you can. Repeat this exercise ten times.

Figure 2

In the *first position*, bring your right leg forward and also lean your body forward as shown in the picture, supporting your left leg on your toes.

Figure 3

Once you are in the position shown in the previous picture, raise your arms very slowly, keeping the left half straight and the right half bent until they reach above your head. Throw them back as far as you can while bringing your right leg back. Then bring your arms and leg back to the same position as in *Figure 2* above and repeat the exercise ten times.

Figure 4

Get into *first position* and move your right leg forward, putting weight on your body from the soles of your feet to your toes. Then raise your right arm with your open hand until it is at shoulder level, as shown in the picture. All this is done at once, taking short steps once you have assumed the position described.

Figure 5

Starting from the position shown in *Figure 4*, place your feet and arms as shown in this picture, remembering to always stand on your toes. Then swing your body to either side until your fingertips touch the ground, alternating your arms. Repeat this exercise ten times.

When you perform the following exercises, all the muscles in the body must be tensed.

Figure 6

Stand in the correct position, that is, the first one, and place your right arm with your open hand, as shown in the picture. Then, very quickly, extend that arm to the right at shoulder level, palm down, while at the same time moving your leg in the same direction (as if you were fencing), imagining that you are hitting something that is in front of you with your fingertips, without thinking of anything else.

Then, also quickly, return to the starting position with your right leg and let your right arm hang along your body. Repeat the same movements with the left side, so that you alternate the exercise.

Figure 7

Stand exactly as shown in the image and prevent your left kneecap from touching the floor. Then move your left leg rapidly forward and place it in the position in which the right leg was, the latter changing at the same time to the position in which the left leg was. Repeat this successively with the left and right leg, and walk in this way through the place where you are.

Figure 8

In the *first position*, raise both arms to the height shown in the figure. Then move the right leg to the left as quickly and forcefully as possible, shifting it as far as possible and returning it to its place. Do the same with the left side to the right side. Repeat this exercise alternately, making sure that the arms are always in the same position.

Figure 9

From the *first position*, walk forward with your right leg and place your arms as shown in the picture. Then very quickly make a semicircle with your arms to the left, making sure that both legs and arms end up in the same position as you move, either to the right or to the left. And do it in such a way that when you move to the left, you maintain the same position as in the picture, only in an inverted position.

Compound exercises

Exercises to be done in the company of another enthusiast.

Figure 10

Both practitioners have to hold the other's right hand, with the right leg in front of them, each slowly pulling the left leg, that is, the leg they had behind them, to the side until it touched the other's leg. While exchanging, remember to always maintain the same intensity of force, both in the arms and in the legs, passing to the left hand of each one, pulling back the right leg, and always pulling each one to his side, as was done with the right hand, and bringing the right leg back into place. Then, instead of shaking hands, they clench and apply pressure with their wrists, repeating the same exercises with the leg movements indicated. Once the movements are repeated, the grip is shifted to the center of the arm and the alternation of legs or arms is repeated as in the previous exercises. As a final exercise, pull each one towards himself with the arm that completed the exercise, and the one with the most strength will carry the other. Then this one will be put to the side and, grabbing the other one by the waist, he will lift his weight so that he can throw him to the ground.

FIGURE 11

Facing each other in the *first position*, both will advance their right leg, and place their right hand on the left side of the other's chest, and their left hand on the wrist of the opponent's right arm. Then bring the bodies together and assume the position shown in the picture.

Figure 12

Once the position in the previous picture has been adopted, both will grab the thigh of the other's right leg with their left hand, and try to lift it off the ground (see picture), which they will prevent by quickly lowering their right arm, with which they break the thigh grip. Then, one by one, they both gradually stand up with arms outstretched and chests together, pushing each other into this position. The stronger one will naturally grab the other, who, bending all the way forward, will give in to the other's momentum, causing him to lose his balance and easily bring him down, grabbing him by the waist with his right arm and throwing him to the ground with his hip.

Practical self-defense techniques

Number 1

This is an arm technique widely used by Japanese police officers. It can be executed in different ways depending on how the opponent's arm is positioned. If it hangs along the body, it is enough to put your arm under the opponent's one, holding the other's hand with one hand, quickly lifting it with both hands, and bending the wrist at the same time, whose twist will dominate him (see photo).

NUMBER 2

Grasp one of your opponent's wrists with one hand in one swift motion and at the same time pull it forcefully toward you. Tilt your body without stiffening it and catch the opponent's arm with your forearm in a lever-like manner, so that it remains below the elbow (as seen in the photo); holding it in the direction of the grabbed arm. The opponent will not be able to do anything with his free hand.

NUMBER 3

Grasp the opponent's hand or wrist as if you were trying to squeeze it, pull it toward you, and try to turn the arm upward. With the other hand, grab the clothing or the tail of the jacket that passes under the arm he is holding, and by applying a slight downward pressure, you can stop the opponent's attack.

Number 4 (1)

Suppose you are attacked and held by the lapel or collar of your clothes, as shown in the picture.

NUMBER 5 (2)

In this case, it is very easy to put the tip of your hand on the wrist of the attacker and with the other grab his elbow, push inward as much as possible, while with the other hand, you push down and pretend to follow the movement with which the other wants to impress you, that is, by luring him to you, you will throw back one leg sharply and, putting all your weight on the wrist of the opponent, you can bring him down.

Number 6 (3)

Another variation of the technique just described. When your opponent reaches for your lapel or collar, grab your opponent's forearm with both hands and try to apply pressure with only your index fingers and thumb. Pull up quickly enough to break the grip and raise your arm to get under your opponent's torso, being careful not to let your opponent's arm block your own head. If you perform the move as quickly as possible, you should be able to pull off the twist as you see it in the picture.

NUMBER 7 (1)

You can easily get rid of the choking of the throat with both hands squeezing the Adam's apple.

It is enough to hit the opponent's groin with one knee or to put both hands together (palm to palm) and raise them to the middle of the opponent's arms with a sudden movement. This movement serves to contain the opponent's pressure on the Adam's apple and facilitate grabbing one of his arms, as we will see in the next technique.

NUMBER 8 (2)

Once the arms are raised as described, grab the other's right arm as shown in the illustration and push it down with the whole body, while the straight leg hits the opponent's knee and brings him down.

NUMBER 9

Also, if the opponent crosses his hands and pulls on the collar or lapel of his clothes with one hand while squeezing his chin with the forearm of the other hand, commonly known as a chokehold, you can simply let go, either with the already known groin knee strike or with what we will explain.

NUMBER 10

Grasp with both hands the wrist of the arm holding the collar or lapel of the garment, and make a violent twist of the body to bring the opponent to the position seen in the picture, from which he will be thrown to the ground with a blow with the leg that is in front of him.

Number 11

If the opponent grabs both your hands by the wrists, you can free yourself with a violent upward movement.

NUMBER 12

Once the arms are raised upwards, as stated earlier, you will quickly grab the forearm of the opponent's right or left hand with both hands, at the same time making a full turn, bringing the arm over the shoulder facing upwards. . From this position, leaning the body forward and holding the arm that is tightly gripped, the opponent can be thrown over the shoulder, easily breaking his arm.

NUMBER 13

If you are holding on in this way, you can release the grip by simply placing your clenched fists on each other's hands.

Number 14

However, if you execute the grip as shown in this picture, with a slight upward movement of the shoulders as you quickly squat, you will let go.

The throw can then be executed at will, either by taking one of your opponent's arms over your shoulder as explained above, or by applying another learned throw.

NUMBER 15

This technique can be applied as a continuation of technique *Number 13*.

Once the opponent has given in, one of his arms is grabbed with both hands and with a sudden upward turn, a half turn of the body backwards, succeeds in preventing his attack.

NUMBER 16 (1)

When it comes to an attack from behind with a cloth or something else, one must not become impatient, no matter how violent the attack, because everything must be done in cold blood.

NUMBER 17 (2)

Then simultaneously turn to the left to trip the attacker's front leg with your right leg and bring him down.

You can then keep him on the ground by simply grabbing the right arm extended upwards so that the elbow is above the knee, used to bridge and push down.

NUMBER 18

A one-handed grip from behind on the neck or clothing is easily released by quickly turning the body and grabbing the opponent's arm at the elbow (see picture) and pushing down. You can finish the technique with a throw, hitting the opponent's leg with the calf muscle.

NUMBER 19

Strikes with the edge of the hand on certain sensitive points, such as the forearm, the upper arm, and the body, are often very effective.

The picture shows how to deflect a blow with a stick with the forearm; while hitting the ribs of the opponent with the edge of the hand and finishing the technique, as we will demonstrate.

NUMBER 20

If you block the first blow and hit it with the edge of your hand in the place shown in the previous picture and block the blow with your forearm, you can easily grab your opponent's stick, which you use in the way shown in this picture.

This technique is not very easy, but if you practice a lot, you can achieve good results with it.

NUMBER 21

Strike the upper part of the elbow with the side of the hand when attacked with a knife or razor and push the armed hand away, then grab the attacker's forearm with the left hand and lean it to the side.

NUMBER 22

Once the blow has been delivered with the side of the hand on the upper part of the elbow, as described in the previous technique, the attacker's arm can be grabbed at the point where the blow was just delivered, and a violent rotation can be executed with both hands. The hands try to interlock the arm in the indicated way. If the pressure is strong enough, this may cause the attacker to drop the weapon.

It is very difficult to perform this technique, so it must be studied carefully.

NUMBER 23

You can also take his hand and give him a strong twist of the wrist to finish the technique, as we'll demonstrate.

NUMBER 24

If, after the previous movement, you deliver an effective blow with the leg the opponent has in front of him, he will be brought down. If the turn continues after he has fallen, he will be forced to drop the weapon.

NUMBER 25

If you are attacked with a knife or other weapon, get as close to the attacker as possible and at the same time grab the armed arm as we have indicated. At the very moment when he raises his arm, you will strike him a powerful blow with your fist on the solar plexus or the pit of the stomach, thus stopping the first movement.

(To be continued).

NUMBER 26

You can finish the previous technique by grasping the forearm, crossing the hand you used to strike the abdomen below the elbow of the arm, grasping the wrist, and pressing down as we demonstrated.

NUMBER 27

This image shows how you can interrupt the first move of a person using a weapon.

With the thumb and forefinger, squeeze the throat shut at the Adam's apple, while with the other hand, a backward twist will be applied at the exact moment the revolver is drawn. Then, when you hit the leg that the opponent has in front of him, he falls on the arm with which the twist was made so that he can no longer shoot.

NUMBER 28

If you are attacked by an assailant wielding a revolver, do not become impatient or agitated. Remain calm and wait for the attacker to begin his task, to which he is giving almost all his attention.

(To be continued).

NUMBER 29

Then, with a quick and precise movement, grab the hand holding the weapon, take it to the side, pull forcefully and at the same time bring the leg in front of the attacker.

(To be continued).

NUMBER 30

Since the opponent loses balance when we grab him by the hand and pull him forcefully to the side, as we demonstrated in the previous technique, it is enough to hit him with the leg placed in front of him in the opponent (see previous picture) to bring him down easily.

As soon as the opponent is on the ground, grab him by the throat with one hand and hold the arm that wields the weapon with the wrist. The most important thing in such a case is not to get nervous and be precise and fast.

NUMBER 31

It is often possible to interrupt an opponent's action by threatening to hit him in the eye, with a newspaper, a hat, or whatever you have at hand.

With this simulated or real threat, he will throw his head back and lose his balance a little, depending on the position he is in, and with a blow with the sole of his foot on his leg, it may be possible to bring him down, depending on how strong the blow turns out to be.

Number 32

With the outside edge of the right hand, you can deliver a blow to the side of an opponent who is about to strike, and with the left hand, you can ward off the body while striking the leg with the sole of the foot.

All these movements will effectively prevent the action of an attacker.

NUMBER 33

The previous technique can also be performed by grabbing one of the opponent's arms by the wrist, twisting and striking with the edge of the hand at the top of the elbow. A well-placed blow can cause certain tendons to dislocate or perhaps break a bone.

NUMBER 34

As a continuation of the previous technique, you can also perform this technique that we will show you.

By pulling the twisted arm downward, and therefore, twisting it tighter, you can bring it down under its own weight or bring it down with a blow to the leg with the sole of the foot. Once he is on the ground, you can squeeze his arm with your knee up to his elbow. You can also easily break his arm.

Number 35

This technique can also be applied as a variant of technique number 32.

You will try to defend the body with both hands and, instead of delivering the blow to the side, hit the side of the knee with the foot, as shown in the picture, which will cause the opponent to fall.

NUMBER 36

If by chance you fall to the ground, you must defend yourself with your feet, as we have demonstrated, and knock your opponent down.

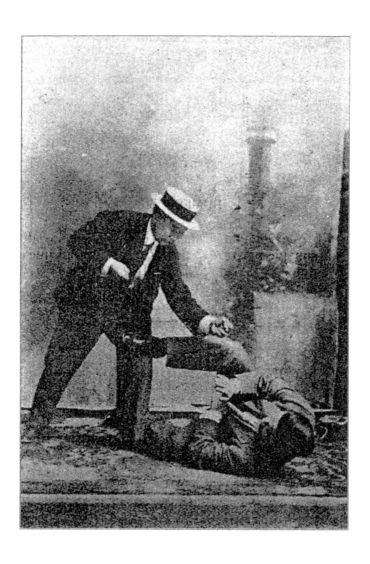

NUMBER 37

Another way to defend yourself on the ground.

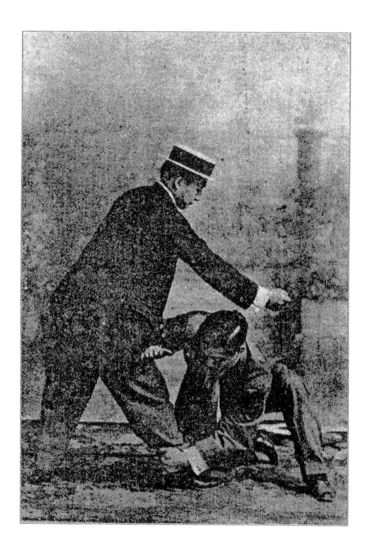

NUMBER 38

When an opponent goes to strike, suddenly crouch down and grab the opponent's front leg (as shown in the picture), pulling one hand toward you while striking with the other. Hit the knee joint, and you will knock him out.

NUMBER 39

Practical way to knock an opponent to the ground while he is trying to punch you in the face by putting his arm around your shoulder.

BREAKFALLS EXERCISES

Think for a moment about the fear most people have of falls and their consequences. Perhaps you have this fear not without reason, because you think that exactly when you fall, a weak part of your body will be damaged, and therefore, depending on the severity of the fall and the injury and the corresponding sensation, you will try to avoid most of the parts of your body hitting the ground and being injured; and exactly in this situation, usually a joint or a sensitive bone receives all the violence of the fall and all the weight of the body with an unpleasant result.

The fear of the fatal consequences of a fall should disappear completely, so by experimenting you will be prepared to partially avoid this fatal outcome. The main thing is to try to stay in a normal state, without getting excited or dizzy, and make sure that the largest part of the body, the fleshy part, not the bony part, hits the ground at the same time. These are usually the parts that hold the momentum and on which the entire weight of the body falls: the palm of the hand, the sole of the foot, and the muscular parts of the legs and arms.

Lying down on a hard floor will be the best way to observe how to get into a good position that allows you to rest comfortably on the muscular or soft parts of the body. To better learn how to use these muscular or fleshy parts of the body, we will present several falling exercises, followed by some keys and throws of Jiu-jitsu, or what is known in Japan as Judo, which is what the Japanese call the modern Jiu-jitsu, as this surname, i.e. jiu-jitsu, was the ancient wrestling used in Japan long before the proclamation of the first emperor Jimmu Tenno and the occupation of the throne in 660 BC.

We can make good use of this Judo demonstration by applying it to the defense we already know.

BREAKFALLS

NUMBER 1

Stand in the position indicated on the picture.

NUMBER 2

Then let yourself fall backwards, making sure that all your hands are touching the floor or the mat at the same time as your back and that your legs are in the position indicated.

Pay attention to the position of the head.

NUMBER 3

Get into the position shown in the picture and support yourself on your right leg.

NUMBER 4

Then let yourself fall backward in the same way as described in *Number 2*, but this time on the left side of the body. Make sure that the sole of the foot and the palm of the hand, as well as the fleshy parts of the arms and legs, hit the ground at the same time as the fallen side of the body.

Make sure that the body rests on the soft parts.

Number 5

Bring your right leg forward and drop forward. As you do so, tuck your chin into your chest and arch your spine as much as you can to shift your entire body weight onto your right shoulder and arm. After the rotation, try to land in the same position as described in *Number 4*.

All of these exercises must be practiced on a padded surface so that you do not injure yourself the first few times. Once learned, they can be performed anywhere.

TAKEDOWNS AND LOCKS

We will now show you some takedowns and locks that you can use for self-defense, as we said.

NUMBER I

This image shows a blow with the sole of the foot on the leg of the opponent in the indicated place, which, supported by a strong impulse with the hands that should hold the clothes of the opponent, goes to the side that you want to bring him down so that he easily loses balance and falls.

Number 2

Pull in by the grip on the opponent's clothes, in order to knock him off balance and strike with the side of the foot on the right side of the thigh, above the knee, to knock him to the ground.

NUMBER 3

Pull him inward to unbalance him, and apply the projection as shown in the picture, that is, you hit it with the calf muscle.

Number 4

Unbalance him in the way already shown, turn quickly to the side, grab the opponent from behind as shown in the picture, and make a sudden movement to the opposite side of the side from which you grab him, to drop him with your hips.

Number 5

Unbalance him in the manner already shown by grabbing the opponent's right arm and taking it over his shoulder, making a corresponding turn so that the opponent is behind you. The arm over the shoulder is pulled down, and by crouching, it is possible to throw the opponent over your head.

NUMBER 6

Get him off balance, grab him by the clothes as we have already shown, drop backwards and place your right foot on the other's stomach with which you lift him into the air, and then pull hard so that he flies over your head, or rather, to throw him.

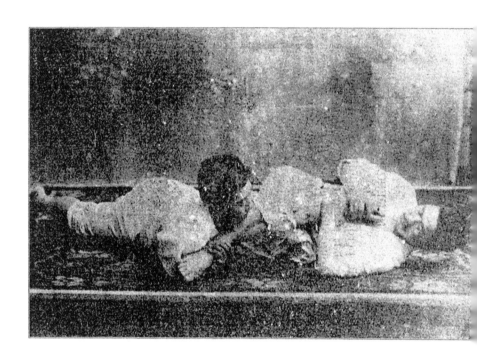

NUMBER 7

This is a very effective armlock. Notice that the arm is twisted upwards, while the right leg is twisted downwards.

NUMBER 8

Another lock or *armbar* on the insides of both legs, with the arm to the side.

Number 9

Armlock, taking advantage of the lapel grip made by the opponent, which will be done by pushing the opponent's arm inward at the elbow.

NUMBER 10

Another armbar, easy to apply.

NUMBER 11

Armbar using the knee while tightening the collar or lapel of the garment.

Number 12

Armbar with leg and body.

NUMBER 13

Chokehold from behind.

Number 14

Another way to apply a chokehold.

NUMBER 15

Leg lock with arms.

This book was composed using the typeface family
Adobe Jenson Pro, with titles in 18-point font, subtitles in
14-point font and text in 11-point font and 14-point spacing,
for Ninety Three, in September 2023.